Learning Python with ChatGPT and Google Colab

The easiest, quickest way to learn Python, using an advanced AI tutor and free cloud tools

Todd Kelsey, PhD
http://linkedin.com/in/tekelsey

TABLE OF CONTENTS

Chapter 1 - Getting Started with Python 3

Chapter 2 - Print Statement and Comments 13

Chapter 3 - Indentation 16

Chapter 4 - Understanding Variables 22

Chapter 5 - Operators 31

Chapter 6 - Functions in Python 35

Chapter 7 - Modules 40

Chapter 8 - Python Libraries 46

Chapter 9 - Numpy 51

Chapter 10 - Basic Data Science Task with Numpy 55

Conclusion 62

Appendix A: Learning Areas in Python 63

Appendix B: Several ChatGPT Tips 65

Chapter 1 - Getting Started with Python

Python is a high-level, interpreted, and general-purpose programming language that was created by Guido van Rossum in 1989 and released in 1991. It emphasizes code readability and simplicity, making it an excellent choice for beginners and experienced programmers alike.

Python is known for its versatile and powerful features, which make it suitable for a wide range of applications. Some of the key uses of Python include:

1. Web Development: Python is commonly used to develop web applications, using frameworks such as Django, Flask, and Pyramid, which enable developers to create server-side applications quickly and efficiently.
2. Data Analysis and Visualization: Python's extensive library ecosystem, including tools like Pandas, NumPy, and Matplotlib, allows for easy data manipulation, analysis, and visualization, making it a popular choice for data scientists and analysts.
3. Machine Learning and Artificial Intelligence: Python is a go-to language for machine learning and AI projects, thanks to libraries like TensorFlow, Keras, and scikit-learn, which provide pre-built algorithms and tools to develop models with ease.
4. Automation and Scripting: Python is often used to automate repetitive tasks or create small scripts for system administration, data processing, and web scraping.
5. Game Development: Python can be used to develop simple games and prototypes using libraries like Pygame and Panda3D.
6. Desktop Applications: Python can be employed to create cross-platform desktop applications with GUI toolkits such as PyQt, Kivy, and Tkinter.
7. Networking and Security: Python's versatility extends to network programming and cybersecurity, with libraries like Scapy, Paramiko, and Requests supporting the development of network tools and security applications.

8. Scientific Computing: The language is used in various scientific domains, including astronomy, physics, and biology, due to libraries like SciPy, Astropy, and BioPython.
9. Blockchain and Cryptocurrency: Python's extensive library support and ease of use make it suitable for developing blockchain applications and working with cryptocurrencies like Bitcoin and Ethereum.
10. Internet of Things (IoT): Python can be used with IoT devices, like Raspberry Pi and Arduino, to build smart devices and automation systems.

Python's extensive library ecosystem, active community, and comprehensive documentation make it an ideal choice for learning and implementing a wide range of projects in various domains.

Set Up Python with Google Colab

Google Colab is a free, cloud-based Jupyter Notebook environment that allows you to write, run, and share Python code easily, without any setup or installation. It's an excellent tool for learning Python quickly, as it provides an interactive environment and access to various libraries and resources. Here's how to get started with Google Colab:

1. Sign in to your Google account: To use Google Colab, you need to have a Google account. If you don't have one, you can create one for free at https://accounts.google.com/signup.
2. Access Google Colab: Visit the Google Colab website at https://colab.research.google.com/. You'll be directed to the welcome page, where you can start using Colab.
3. Create a new notebook: Click on "File" in the top-left menu and select "New notebook" to create a new Jupyter Notebook. A new tab will open with an empty notebook where you can start writing Python code.
4. Familiarize yourself with the interface: A Google Colab notebook consists of cells, which can be either code cells or text cells. Code

cells allow you to write and execute Python code, while text cells let you add formatted text, images, and equations using Markdown.
5. Write Python code: Click on the first cell in the notebook and start typing Python code. When you're ready to execute the code, press Shift + Enter or click on the "Play" button to the left of the cell. The output will appear below the cell.
6. Add more cells: To add a new cell, hover your mouse between cells or at the bottom of the last cell. Click on the "+ Code" button to add a code cell or the "+ Text" button to add a text cell.
7. Save your notebook: Google Colab automatically saves your notebook to your Google Drive while you're working. However, you can also click on "File" and select "Save" or "Save a copy in Drive" to ensure your work is saved.
8. Import libraries: You can import Python libraries by writing `import` statements in a code cell, just like you would in a regular Python script. Many popular libraries, like NumPy, Pandas, and Matplotlib, come pre-installed with Google Colab.
9. Share your notebook: To share your notebook with others, click on the "Share" button in the top-right corner. You can invite people via email or generate a shareable link with various access permissions.
10. Explore tutorials and examples: Google Colab offers a variety of pre-built notebooks to help you learn Python and explore various libraries and concepts. Click on "File" and select "Open notebook" to browse the available options.

Google Colab is an excellent platform to quickly start learning Python and experiment with code in an interactive environment. As you progress, you can use Colab to explore advanced topics, such as machine learning, data visualization, and more.

Running Your First Python Script with Google Colab

(Google Colab Recap: Google Colab is a cloud-based service provided by Google that allows you to write, run, and share Python code through Jupyter Notebooks. It provides free access to computing resources, making it an excellent choice for running Python scripts, especially if you don't want to install Python on your local machine.)

Here's how you can run your first Python script using Google Colab:

Open Google Colab:

1. Go to https://colab.research.google.com/ and sign in with your Google account.

Create a new notebook:

2. Click on "File" in the top-left corner, and then click on "New notebook." A new Jupyter Notebook will open in your browser.

Rename the notebook:

3. Click on the default notebook name "Untitled0.ipynb" at the top-left corner, and give it a meaningful name like "My_First_Python_Script.ipynb."

Write a Python script:

4. In the first cell of the notebook, you can write a simple Python script, like the classic "Hello, World!" program. Type the following code:

    ```
    print("Hello, World!")
    ```

Run the script:

5. Press "Shift+Enter" or click the "Play" button on the left side of the cell to run the script. The output "Hello, World!" will be displayed below the cell.

Add more cells and code:

6. Click on the "+ Code" button at the top-left corner to add more cells to the notebook. You can write and run more Python code as you need.

Save the notebook:

7. Google Colab automatically saves your notebook to Google Drive as you work on it, but you can also manually save by clicking "File" and then "Save" or "Save a copy in Drive."

Share the notebook:

8. If you want to share your notebook with others, click on the "Share" button at the top-right corner, and then you can either invite people via email or generate a shareable link.

That's it! You've successfully created and run your first Python script using Google Colab. You can now continue to explore more complex Python code and even utilize the powerful GPU resources provided by Google Colab for machine learning and data analysis tasks.

Learning Python with ChatGPT

ChatGPT can help you learn Python in several ways. As an AI language model, it can provide explanations, answer questions, and offer guidance on various Python-related topics. Here are some ways ChatGPT can assist you in learning Python:

1. Concept explanations: ChatGPT can provide detailed explanations of Python concepts, ranging from basic to advanced topics, such as data types, loops, functions, classes, and more.
2. Code examples: ChatGPT can generate code snippets to demonstrate how to use Python features, libraries, and packages. These examples can serve as a starting point for your own projects or help you understand how to implement specific functionality.
3. Debugging assistance: If you're facing issues with your Python code, ChatGPT can help identify and suggest solutions to fix common errors and issues.
4. Best practices: ChatGPT can provide guidance on Python best practices, such as coding style, variable naming conventions, and code organization.
5. Library and package recommendations: ChatGPT can recommend useful Python libraries and packages for various tasks, such as data manipulation, web development, machine learning, and more.
6. Project ideas: If you're looking for inspiration or ideas for Python projects, ChatGPT can suggest project ideas based on your interests or skill level.
7. Learning resources: ChatGPT can recommend Python learning resources, such as online tutorials, courses, books, or documentation, to help you deepen your understanding of Python.

To get the most out of ChatGPT while learning Python, feel free to ask specific questions, request examples or explanations, and seek guidance on the topics you need help with. By engaging in interactive conversations with ChatGPT, you can enhance your Python knowledge and strengthen your programming skills.

Accessing ChatGPT

Visit https://chat.openai.com/chat and either login or signup.

Note: At the time of writing, Version 3.5 is free, and reasonably capable, with some usage limits. It is possible it can be overloaded at time because of the popularity. Version 4 is more capable, and has a monthly cost. It's definitely worth it. In addition to being able to help you learn

Python, ChatGPT is increasingly becoming a desired skill in the workplace. It can be used for a great variety of functions.

Examples: https://www.theycallmehoz.com/chat-gpt-examples

Chapter 2 - Print Statement and Comments

Python Print statement

The "Hello World" exercise is a classic way to start coding, and it is easy to do in Google Colab.

1. Open Google Colab by visiting the following link: https://colab.research.google.com/
2. Click on the "File" menu in the top-left corner, and then click on "New notebook" to create a new notebook.
3. You should now see an empty cell in your notebook. Click inside the cell to start editing.
4. Type the following code in the cell:

print("Hello, World!")

5. To run the code, press "Shift + Enter" on your keyboard or click the play button (▶) on the left side of the cell. This will execute the code and display the output below the cell.

Hello, World!

Congratulations! You've successfully created and run a "Hello, World!" statement in Google Colab. You can continue to add new cells and write more Python code to explore and learn further.

Comments in Python

Comments are lines of text in your code that are not executed by the Python interpreter. They're useful for explaining your code, making it easier for others to understand or for reminding yourself of what your code does. In Python, you can write comments in two ways:

a. Single-line comments:

Single-line comments start with the # symbol. The Python interpreter ignores everything after the # symbol on that line. Here's an example of a single-line comment in a Google **Colab cell:**

This is a single-line comment print("Hello, World!") # This comment is on the same line as the code

b. Multi-line comments:

Multi-line comments are used to write comments that span multiple lines. You can create a multi-line comment by enclosing the text between triple quotes (''' or """). Here's an example of a multi-line comment in a Google Colab cell:

''' This is a multi-line comment. It can span multiple lines. ''' print("Hello, World!")

Remember that multi-line comments using triple quotes are not true comments but rather multi-line strings that are not assigned to a variable. The Python interpreter will still process them, but they won't have any effect on your code execution.

Chapter 3 - Indentation

Indentation is an essential aspect of Python programming. It is used to define the structure of code blocks, which helps maintain code readability and clarity. Unlike other programming languages that use braces (curly brackets) {} to indicate code blocks, Python relies on indentation.

Here are some essential points to understand indentation in Python:

1. Code blocks: Indentation is used to create code blocks, such as loops, conditional statements, and function or class definitions. A consistent amount of space or tabs should be used to indicate a new level of indentation. The recommended practice is to use 4 spaces for each level of indentation.
2. Consistency: It's essential to be consistent with the type and number of indentation characters used throughout the code. Mixing tabs and spaces or using a different number of spaces for indentation levels can lead to errors or unexpected behavior.
3. Indentation Errors: Python will raise an `IndentationError` if the code is not correctly indented. This usually occurs when the indentation is inconsistent or when a code block is not indented at all.

Here's a simple example using several print statements to demonstrate the use of indentation in Python:

```python
# Define a list of numbers
numbers = [1, 2, 3]


# Print the start message
print("Starting the loop...")


# Iterate through the list of numbers using a for loop
```

```python
for number in numbers:
    # This line is indented to show it is inside the 'for' loop
    print(f"Current number: {number}")

    # Check if the number is even
    if number % 2 == 0:
        # This line is indented to show it is inside the 'if' statement
        print(f"{number} is even")
    else:
        # This line is indented to show it is inside the 'else' statement
        print(f"{number} is odd")

    # This line is indented to show it is inside the 'for' loop
    print("Loop iteration complete")

# Print the end message
print("Finished the loop")
```

In this example, we have several print statements, and indentation is used to indicate their position within code blocks:

1. The `print("Starting the loop...")` and `print("Finished the loop")` statements are outside the `for` loop, so they are not indented.
2. The `print(f"Current number: {number}")` and `print("Loop iteration complete")` statements are inside the `for` loop, so they are indented to the same level as the `if` and `else` statements.
3. The `print(f"{number} is even")` statement is inside the `if` statement, so it is indented one level further than the `if` statement.

4. The `print(f"{number} is odd")` statement is inside the `else` statement, so it is indented one level further than the `else` statement.

This example demonstrates how indentation is used to define the structure of code blocks in Python and helps maintain code readability.

Try it In Google Colab

To run the provided code in Google Colab, follow these steps:
1. Open Google Colab: Go to https://colab.research.google.com/ and sign in with your Google account.
2. Create a new notebook: Click on "File" in the menu and then select "New notebook." This will create a new Python notebook where you can write and execute code.
3. Write the code: In the first cell of the notebook, copy and paste the code from the example:

```python
# Define a list of numbers
numbers = [1, 2, 3]

# Print the start message
print("Starting the loop...")

# Iterate through the list of numbers using a for loop
for number in numbers:
    # This line is indented to show it is inside the 'for' loop
    print(f"Current number: {number}")

    # Check if the number is even
    if number % 2 == 0:
        # This line is indented to show it is inside the 'if' statement
        print(f"{number} is even")
    else:
        # This line is indented to show it is inside the 'else' statement
        print(f"{number} is odd")

    # This line is indented to show it is inside the 'for' loop
    print("Loop iteration complete")
```

\# Print the end message
print("Finished the loop")

4. **Run the cell: Press** `Shift + Enter` **or click the play button to the left of the cell to execute the code. The output should display:**

Starting the loop...
Current number: 1
1 is odd
Loop iteration complete
Current number: 2
2 is even
Loop iteration complete
Current number: 3
3 is odd
Loop iteration complete
Finished the loop

This output demonstrates that the code has been executed successfully in Google Colab. You can now experiment with the code, modify it, or add more cells to your notebook as needed.

Chapter 4 - Understanding Variables

Variables in Python are essential building blocks for writing programs. They are used to store data and make it accessible to the code. Here's a brief overview of what you need to know about variables in Python:

1. Variable declaration and assignment: In Python, you can declare a variable and assign a value to it using the assignment operator (=). Python is a dynamically-typed language, which means that you don't need to specify the data type when declaring a variable.

x = 10 name = "Alice"

2. Variable naming: Variables should have descriptive names to make the code more readable. In Python, variable names can consist of letters, numbers, and underscores, but they cannot start with a number. By convention, variable names are written in lowercase, with words separated by underscores.

Good variable names age = 30 first_name = "John" # Bad variable names 1st_name = "John" # Starts with a number

3. Data types: Python has several built-in data types for variables, such as integers, floats, strings, lists, tuples, dictionaries, and sets. The type of a variable is determined automatically based on the assigned value.

integer_variable = 42 float_variable = 3.14 string_variable = "Hello, World!"

4. Variable scope: Variables in Python have a scope that defines their accessibility within the code. There are two main types of variable scopes: global and local. Global variables are accessible throughout the code, while local variables are accessible only within the function or block of code where they are defined.

global_var = "I am global" def my_function(): local_var = "I am local" print(global_var) print(local_var) my_function() # Output: I am global / I am local print(global_var) # Output: I am global print(local_var) # Error: local_var is not defined outside the function

5. Basic operations: You can use variables to perform basic operations like addition, subtraction, multiplication, division, etc. You can also use variables to perform comparisons and logical operations.

a = 10 b = 20 sum = a + b difference = a - b product = a * b quotient = a / b is_equal = a == b is_greater = a > b

6. Data structures: Variables can store different types of data structures, such as lists, tuples, dictionaries, and sets. These data structures can be used to store and manipulate collections of data.

my_list = [1, 2, 3, 4, 5] my_tuple = (1, 2, 3) my_dict = {'key1': 'value1', 'key2': 'value2'} my_set = {1, 2, 3, 4}

Understanding variables in Python is essential for programming, as they allow you to store and manipulate data throughout your code.

Hands-On Exercise - Google Colab

Here's a simple hands-on exercise with variables in Google Colab. This exercise will help you get familiar with declaring variables, performing operations, and displaying results in Colab.

1. Step 1: Open Google Colab by visiting https://colab.research.google.com and sign in with your Google

account. Create a new Python 3 notebook by clicking on "File" > "New notebook".
2. Step 2: In the first code cell, declare two variables a and b and assign them integer values:

```
a = 5 b = 10
```

Run the cell by clicking the play button or pressing Shift + Enter.

3. Step 3: In the second code cell, perform arithmetic operations using the variables a and b, and display the results:

```
sum_ab = a + b difference_ab = a - b product_ab = a * b quotient_ab = a / b print("Sum:", sum_ab) print("Difference:", difference_ab) print("Product:", product_ab) print("Quotient:", quotient_ab)
```

Run the cell to see the results of the operations.

4. Step 4: In the third code cell, declare a list containing integers and calculate their average:

```
numbers = [1, 2, 3, 4, 5, 6, 7, 8, 9, 10] sum_numbers = sum(numbers) average = sum_numbers / len(numbers) print("Average:", average)
```

Run the cell to display the average of the numbers in the list.

5. Step 5: In the fourth code cell, create a simple dictionary containing names and ages, and display a person's age using their name as a key:

```
people = { 'Alice': 30, 'Bob': 25, 'Charlie': 22 } name = 'Alice' age = people[name] print(f"{name}'s age is {age}")
```

Run the cell to display the age of the person with the specified name.

This exercise should give you a basic understanding of how to work with variables in Google Colab. You can continue exploring Python and Colab by adding more code cells and experimenting with different variable types, data structures, and operations.

Hands-On Exercise - ChatGPT

Access ChatGPT at: https://chat.openai.com/chat

Try the something like the following prompt:

Write a very short program in python that uses variables, and explain what the variable is doing.

The output will look something like this:

Here's a short Python program that uses variables:

```python
a = 5
b = 10
sum = a + b
print("The sum of a and b is:", sum)
```

Explanation:

1. `a = 5`: Here, we're creating a variable named 'a' and assigning it the value 5. This stores the integer value 5 in the memory location associated with the variable 'a'.
2. `b = 10`: Similarly, we create another variable named 'b' and assign it the value 10.
3. `sum = a + b`: We create a new variable named 'sum' and assign it the value of 'a' added to the value of 'b' (5 + 10).
4. `print("The sum of a and b is:", sum)`: We use the print function to display a message and the value of the 'sum' variable, which is 15 in this case. The output will be "The sum of a and b is: 15".

If you want to try running the code, you could copy it from ChatGPT and paste it into a Google Colab Notebook. On a mobile device, there are also apps called Python IDE's (integrated python environments), such as Pythonista and others, where you can type code or copy and run it easily.

To copy the code from ChatGPT, try selecting the Copy Code button:

Here's a short Python program that uses variables:

```python
a = 5
b = 10
sum = a + b
print("The sum of a and b is:", sum)
```

Running the Code in Google Colab

1. Go to https://colab.research.google.com/ and sign in with your Google account.
2. Click on "File" in the top-left corner, and then click "New notebook" to create a new Colab notebook.
3. In the new notebook, you will see a code cell. Copy and paste the Python code from ChatGPT (in a separate window or tab) into Google Colab.
4. Press Shift + Enter or click the play button to the left of the code cell to run the code. The output should appear below the cell, displaying "The sum of a and b is: 15".

If you need to make any changes to the code or run it again, simply edit the code in the cell and press Shift + Enter or click the play button once more.

Chapter 5 - Operators

In Python, operators are special symbols that are used to perform various operations on variables and values.

These operators can be categorized into several types. This list includes some of the most commonly used operators:

1. Arithmetic Operators:
    - Addition (+): Adds two values.
    - Subtraction (-): Subtracts the right operand from the left operand.
    - Multiplication (*): Multiplies two values.
    - Division (/): Divides the left operand by the right operand.
2. Comparison Operators:
    - Equal (==): Returns True if the two operands are equal.
    - Not equal (!=): Returns True if the two operands are not equal.
    - Greater than (>): Returns True if the left operand is greater than the right operand.
    - Less than (<): Returns True if the left operand is less than the right operand.
    - Greater than or equal to (>=): Returns True if the left operand is greater than or equal to the right operand.
    - Less than or equal to (<=): Returns True if the left operand is less than or equal to the right operand.
3. Logical Operators:
    - and: Returns True if both the operands are true.
    - or: Returns True if either of the operands is true.
    - not: Returns True if the operand is false.
4. Bitwise Operators:
    - Bitwise AND (&): Performs bitwise AND operation on the corresponding bits of the operands.
    - Bitwise OR (|): Performs bitwise OR operation on

Simple Code Example

Below is a simple code example that can enter into Google Colab. (To copy this specific code, you can get it from http://learnskills.tech, or you could also ask ChatGPT for an example, with a prompt like: Simple code example using operators in python – and then copy the code into Google Colab and run it.)

```
# addition
num1 = 10
num2 = 5
result = num1 + num2
print("The sum of", num1, "and", num2, "is", result)

# subtraction
num3 = 20
num4 = 8
result2 = num3 - num4
print("The difference between", num3, "and", num4, "is", result2)

# multiplication
num5 = 5
num6 = 6
result3 = num5 * num6
print("The product of", num5, "and", num6, "is", result3)

# division
num7 = 15
num8 = 3
result4 = num7 / num8
print("The quotient of", num7, "and", num8, "is", result4)
```

And the output will look something like this:

The sum of 10 and 5 is 15
The difference between 20 and 8 is 12
The product of 5 and 6 is 30
The quotient of 15 and 3 is 5.0

Additional Operators

These are some additional operators that not as common but can be important in some situations.

1. Arithmetic Operators:
    - Modulus (%): Returns the remainder of the division.
    - Exponentiation (**): Raises the left operand to the power of the right operand.
    - Floor Division (//): Performs division and returns the largest whole number less than or equal to the result.
2. Logical Operators:
    - and: Returns True if both the operands are true.
    - or: Returns True if either of the operands is true.
    - not: Returns True if the operand is false.
3. Bitwise Operators:
    - Bitwise AND (&): Performs bitwise AND operation on the corresponding bits of the operands.
    - Bitwise OR (|): Performs bitwise OR operation on

Chapter 6 - Functions in Python

In Python, functions are blocks of reusable code that are designed to perform a specific task. Functions can be useful for breaking down complex tasks into smaller, manageable parts, as well as for reusing code in different parts of your program. Here's an overview of how to define and use functions in Python.

Defining a function:

To define a function in Python, you use the `def` keyword, followed by the function name, parentheses, and a colon. The code block that follows, indented by 4 spaces or a tab, represents the function body. Functions can take input arguments, which are placed within the parentheses, and can return a value using the `return` statement.

Here's an example of a simple function that takes two arguments and returns their sum:

```python
def add_numbers(a, b): result = a + b return result
```

Calling a function:

To call a function, use its name followed by parentheses, with any required arguments inside. Here's an example of how to call the `add_numbers` function defined earlier:

```python
sum = add_numbers(3, 5) print(sum) # Output: 8
```

Default argument values:

You can provide default values for function arguments by using the assignment operator (=) in the function definition. This allows you to call the function with fewer arguments than it has parameters, as the default values will be used for any missing arguments.

```
def greet(name, greeting="Hello"): return f"{greeting}, {name}!"

print(greet("John")) # Output: Hello, John! print(greet("
```

Try in Google Colab

To try the example code in Google Colab, follow these steps:
1) Open Google Colab by visiting https://colab.research.google.com/
2) Click on 'File' in the top left corner, and then click on 'New Notebook' to create a new notebook.
3) Copy and paste the code into separate code cells in the notebook.
4) Try runing each cell by clicking the play button or pressing `Shift + Enter`.

Try ChatGPT

1) Access ChatGPT https://chat.openai.com/chat
2) Enter a prompt like this into ChatGPT:
Write an example of Python code that uses functions
or
Write an example of Python code that uses functions. Ask users to choose a sandwich or bowl of vegetable soup and then list the ingredients

3) Try copying the code from ChatGPT into Google Colab and running it.

Debugging in ChatGPT

Debugging is a very helpful option when you are learning to code or working on any project. When you are working on code, if you have problems, tell ChatGPT if it didn't work. (Sometimes ChatGPT makes mistakes). Humans also make mistakes, and if you customize code or try writing a program, and run it, if there is a problem try asking ChatGPT to evaluate your code and in the same prompt, enter your code.

Try ChatGPT > Resources

Try asking ChatGPT to recommend some resources for learning more about Functions in Python, such as videos, tutorials or hands on exercises.

Return statements in Functions with variables

In Python, the `return` statement is used to send a result back from a function to the caller. You can return variables, expressions, or values directly. Here are some examples of using return statements with variables:

Example 1: Return a single variable

def add(a, b): result = a + b return result sum = add(3, 5) print(sum) # Output: 8

Example 2: Return multiple variables as a dictionary

def get_student_info(student_id): student_data = { 101: {"name": "Alice", "age": 20, "grade": "A"}, 102: {"name": "Bob", "age": 21, "grade": "B"}, } return student_data.get(student_id, "Student not found") student_info = get_student_info(101) print(student_info) # Output: {'name': 'Alice', 'age': 20, 'grade': 'A'}

In each of these examples, the `return` statement is used to send the result of the computation back to the caller, which can then be stored

(Try in Google Colab, ask ChatGPT for more examples)

Chapter 7 - Modules

Python is a versatile and powerful programming language that uses a modular approach to organizing code. Modules in Python are simply files containing Python code, usually with a .py extension. They can include functions, classes, and variables that can be imported and used in other Python scripts.

There are many built-in Python modules that come with the standard library, as well as third-party modules that can be installed using package managers like pip or conda.

Here are some commonly used Python modules:

Built-in Modules:
a. math: Provides mathematical functions like trigonometric, logarithmic, and others.
b. os: Offers a way to interact with the operating system, e.g., file handling, process management.
c. sys: Enables access to system-specific parameters and functions.
d. re: Supports regular expressions for text processing and manipulation.
e. datetime: Supplies classes for working with dates and times.
f. random: Contains functions to generate random numbers.
g. json: Allows encoding and decoding JSON data.
h. collections: Implements specialized container datatypes like namedtuple, defaultdict, and Counter.

ChatGPT:
Try asking ChatGPT for more information, resources or examples on anything you don't recognize or want to learn more about.

To use a module in your Python code, you need to import it first. You can import a module using the `import` statement, followed by the module name:

import module_name

You can also import specific functions, classes, or variables from a module using the `from ... import ...` statement:

from module_name import function_name, class_name, variable_name

Additionally, you can use aliases to shorten module names or avoid naming conflicts:

import module_name as alias_name

Example - 're' Module

The `re` module in Python is used for working with regular expressions, which are powerful tools for text processing and manipulation. Here's a simple example that demonstrates the use of the `re` module to find all email addresses in a given text:

import re

# Sample text containing email addresses
text = "Please send your queries to support@example.com and sales@example.org."

# Regular expression pattern to match email addresses
email_pattern = r'\b[A-Za-z0-9._%+-]+@[A-Za-z0-9.-]+\.[A-Z|a-z]{2,}\b'

Find all email addresses in the text using the re.findall() method email_addresses = re.findall(email_pattern, text)

Print the list of email addresses found

```
print(email_addresses)
```

Output:

['support@example.com', 'sales@example.org']

In this example, the `re.findall()` function is used to find all non-overlapping occurrences of the email pattern in the given text. The email pattern is defined using a regular expression, and the resulting list of matched email addresses is printed.

Try in Google Colab

To try the example code in Google Colab, follow these steps:
1. Open Google Colab by visiting https://colab.research.google.com/
2. Click on 'File' in the top left corner, and then click on 'New Notebook' to create a new notebook.
3. Copy and paste the code into separate code cells in the notebook.
4. Try running each cell by clicking the play button or pressing Shift + Enter.

ChatGPT

Want to learn more about using regular expressions and what they are? Ask ChatGPT to explain, and ask it for resources to learn more. If it gives you an example that feels too complex, try asking it for a simpler example.

Another interesting question to ask would be for the most common uses of _____ (module, library, etc.)

Modules and Libraries

The next chapter covers Python libraries.

In Python, a module is a single file that contains Python definitions, including functions, classes, and variables. On the other hand, a library is a collection of modules that are related and packaged together for a specific purpose.

Here are some key differences between modules and libraries in Python:

1. Scope: A module is typically used to organize related functionality within a single file, while a library is used to organize related functionality across multiple files.
2. Functionality: A module typically provides a set of related functions, classes, and variables that can be used in other parts of the code, while a library provides a broader range of functionality, often spanning multiple domains.
3. Usage: A module can be imported and used in other Python scripts or modules, while a library is typically installed and used as a third-party package.
4. Dependency: A module may or may not have dependencies on other modules or libraries, while a library usually has dependencies on other libraries or modules.

In summary, modules are used to organize related functionality within a single file, while libraries are used to organize related functionality across multiple files and provide a broader range of functionality.

Chapter 8 - Python Libraries

Python libraries allow you to perform advanced functions by simply using them, instead of having to write your code from scratch.

A Python library is a collection of modules that are designed to be reused in various Python programs. A library is essentially a package of pre-written code that can be imported into a Python script, providing a set of functions, classes, and methods that can be used to perform specific tasks without having to write the code from scratch.

Python libraries are typically written in Python, although some libraries may include code written in other programming languages for performance or compatibility reasons. Libraries can range from general-purpose libraries, such as NumPy and Pandas for data analysis, to specialized libraries for specific tasks, such as Pygame for game development or Flask for web development.

Python libraries are typically distributed and installed using package managers such as pip or conda. Once a library is installed, it can be imported into a Python script using the import statement, and its functions, classes, and methods can be used as needed within the script.

Overall, Python libraries provide a way to save time and effort by leveraging pre-existing code to perform tasks, making it easier for developers to write Python programs.

Popular Libraries

Python has a rich ecosystem of libraries that provide developers with a variety of functionalities to build their applications. Here are some popular Python libraries:

1. NumPy: A library for numerical computing in Python. It provides a powerful N-dimensional array object and tools for working with these arrays.
2. Pandas: A library for data manipulation and analysis. It provides tools for reading and writing data in various formats, data cleaning, and data transformation.
3. Matplotlib: A library for creating visualizations in Python. It provides a wide range of plots, including line charts, scatter plots, and bar charts.
4. Scikit-learn: A library for machine learning in Python. It provides tools for classification, regression, clustering, and dimensionality reduction.
5. TensorFlow: A library for building and training deep learning models. It provides tools for creating neural networks and performing operations on large datasets.
6. Pygame: A library for game development in Python. It provides tools for building games with graphics, sound, and user input.
7. Requests: A library for making HTTP requests in Python. It provides a simple API for interacting with web services and APIs.
8. Beautiful Soup: A library for web scraping in Python. It provides tools for parsing HTML and XML documents and extracting data from them.
9. Flask: A lightweight web framework for building web applications in Python. It provides tools for handling requests, building templates, and managing sessions.
10. Django: A full-stack web framework for building web applications in Python. It provides tools for handling requests, building templates, managing databases, and handling user authentication.

Using Libraries in Google Colab

Running Python locally on your laptop or PC is a very common way of using Python, but it involves having to install Python, and package managers like PIP mentioned above. Eventually you'll probably want to use "local Python", but installing libraries can be time consuming. When you're getting started, Google Colab is a great place to start, and can save you time and hassle.

Google Colab is a cloud-based environment for running Jupyter notebooks that allows users to use Python libraries without having to install them locally on their computers. Here are the steps to use libraries in Google Colab:

1. Open a new or existing Jupyter notebook in Google Colab.
2. To install a library, use the !pip install command followed by the name of the library. For example, to install the NumPy library, run the following command in a code cell:

!pip install numpy

3. After the installation is complete, you can import the library using the import statement in the same code cell or subsequent cells. For example, to import NumPy, use the following statement:

import numpy as np

4. Once the library is imported, you can use its functions and classes in the notebook.

Note that some libraries may require additional dependencies or configurations, which can be installed or set up using the appropriate commands. Also, Google Colab may require users to restart the runtime environment after installing certain libraries before they can be used in the notebook. This can be done by clicking on the Runtime menu and selecting Restart runtime.

Chapter 9 - Numpy

NumPy is a Python library used for numerical computing, including data science and machine learning. It provides support for multi-dimensional arrays and matrices, as well as a large collection of mathematical functions for working with these arrays. NumPy is used extensively in scientific computing, data analysis, and machine learning applications.

Benefit: like many other math related libraries, Numpy gives you the ability to accomplish a significant amount where math is needed, without necessarily having to learn all the related math.

Some of the key features of NumPy include:

- ndarray: A multi-dimensional array object that is the backbone of NumPy. It allows for fast operations on large arrays and provides a convenient way to store and manipulate data.
- Broadcasting: A set of rules that allows for element-wise operations between arrays of different shapes and sizes, without requiring the arrays to be of the same shape.
- Mathematical functions: A large collection of mathematical functions for performing common operations like trigonometry, logarithms, exponentials, and more.
- Linear algebra: NumPy provides support for a wide range of linear algebra functions, such as matrix multiplication, eigenvalue decomposition, and singular value decomposition.
- Fourier analysis: NumPy provides support for Fourier analysis, which is a mathematical technique used for analyzing periodic functions and signals.

Overall, NumPy is a powerful and versatile library that is essential for many scientific computing and data analysis tasks in Python.

Numpy Example

Here's an example of using NumPy for a basic data science task - computing the mean and standard deviation of a set of data.

First, we'll start by importing NumPy:

import numpy as np

Next, let's create an array of data. For this example, we'll use a random array of 1000 numbers:

data = np.random.randn(1000)

(Tip: Try asking ChatGPT what an array is.)

Now, we can use NumPy functions to compute the mean and standard deviation of this data:

mean = np.mean(data) std_dev = np.std(data)

Finally, we can print out the results:

print("Mean: ", mean) print("Standard deviation: ", std_dev)

This will output the mean and standard deviation of the data we generated. Of course, in a real data science task, you would likely be working with real-world data, but the basic approach would be the same - load your data into a NumPy array and use NumPy functions to perform calculations on that data.

(Tip: Try asking ChatGPT what mean and standard deviation are and to give real world examples of how they are used in business.)

Try in Google Colab

To try the example code in Google Colab, follow these steps:
1. Open Google Colab by visiting https://colab.research.google.com/
2. Click on 'File' in the top left corner, and then click on 'New Notebook' to create a new notebook.

3. Copy and paste the code into separate code cells in the notebook.
4. Try running each cell by clicking the play button or pressing Shift + Enter.

Chapter 10 - Basic Data Science Task with Numpy

Here's an example of using NumPy for a basic data science task - computing the mean and standard deviation of a set of data.

First, we'll start by importing NumPy:

import numpy as np

Next, let's create an array of data. For this example, we'll use a random array of 1000 numbers:

data = np.random.randn(1000)

Now, we can use NumPy functions to compute the mean and standard deviation of this data:

mean = np.mean(data) std_dev = np.std(data)

Finally, we can print out the results:

print("Mean: ", mean) print("Standard deviation: ", std_dev)

This will output the mean and standard deviation of the data we generated. Of course, in a real data science task, you would likely be working with real-world data, but the basic approach would be the same - load your data into a NumPy array and use NumPy functions to perform calculations on that data.

Google Colab and Numpy

Using Google Colab, you can work in the cloud, even when you need to load a data file.

NumPy can be used in Google Colab for loading data from files and performing advanced tasks. In fact, Google Colab provides a great platform for working with NumPy, as it comes pre-installed with the library and provides access to powerful hardware resources.

To load data from a file in Google Colab, you can use the same NumPy functions that you would use in a local Python environment. For example, you might use `loadtxt` to load a CSV file:

import numpy as np # Load data from CSV file
data = np.loadtxt('data.csv', delimiter=',')

In this example, `data.csv` is a CSV file in the current working directory of the Colab environment. You can also specify the full path to the file if it's located elsewhere.

Once you have loaded your data into a NumPy array, you can use all of the powerful functions provided by the library to perform advanced data analysis and manipulation tasks. For example, you might use NumPy's linear algebra functions to perform a principal component analysis (PCA) on your data:

Perform PCA on data from numpy
.linalg import svd
U, S, V = svd(data)

Tip: Ask ChatGPT for examples of how linear algebra is used in data science, and for resources to learn more about linear algebra for data science, and PCA (principal component analysis). You can also ask ChatGPT to help you learn linear algebra; Khan Academy is also working on incorporating GPT technology into learning materials and is worth checking into.

This is just a simple example, but NumPy provides many more advanced functions for working with arrays and performing complex computations. Google Colab provides a great environment for exploring these functions and working with large datasets.

Google Colab: Placing a Data File for use with Numpy

To place a data file in the working directory of a Google Colab notebook, you can use the file upload feature in the notebook interface. Here's how to do it:

1. Open your Google Colab notebook and make sure you're in the "Files" tab in the left-hand sidebar.
2. Click on the "Upload" button and select the file you want to upload from your local machine.
3. Once the file has finished uploading, you should see it listed in the "Files" tab. You can also verify that it's in the working directory by running `!ls` in a code cell and checking the output.

Now that the file is in the working directory, you can use NumPy functions to load it into an array, as I showed in my previous answer. For example, if you uploaded a CSV file called `data.csv`, you could load it into a NumPy array like this:

import numpy as np # Load data from CSV file

```
data = np.loadtxt('data.csv', delimiter=',')
```

This assumes that the CSV file has comma-separated values. If the file has a different delimiter, you can specify it using the `delimiter` argument of `loadtxt`.

Example: using NumPy in Google Colab

This example shows how to load a sample data file and perform some basic computations on it:

1. First, we need to place the data file in the working directory. For this example, we'll use the Iris dataset, which is a popular dataset for machine learning tasks. You can download the file from the UCI Machine Learning Repository at this URL: https://archive.ics.uci.edu/ml/datasets/iris. Save the file as `iris.csv` on your local machine.
2. Next, upload the `iris.csv` file to the working directory of your Google Colab notebook using the file upload feature in the notebook interface. You can do this by clicking on the "Files" tab in the left-hand sidebar, then clicking on the "Upload" button and selecting the `iris.csv` file from your local machine.
3. Once the file has been uploaded, we can use NumPy to load it into an array and perform some basic computations on it. Here's an example:

```
import numpy as np


# Load data from CSV file

data = np.loadtxt('iris.csv', delimiter=',', usecols=(0, 1, 2, 3))


# Compute mean and standard deviation of each column

mean = np.mean(data, axis=0)

std_dev = np.std(data, axis=0)
```

```
# Print results
print("Mean: ", mean)
print("Standard deviation: ", std_dev)
```

In this example, we first load the data from the `iris.csv` file using `loadtxt`, specifying the delimiter as a comma and selecting the first four columns of data using the `usecols` argument. We then compute the mean and standard deviation of each column using NumPy's `mean` and `std` functions, and print out the results.

Note that this is just a simple example of using NumPy in Google Colab with a sample data file. NumPy provides many more advanced functions for working with arrays and performing complex computations, and Google Colab provides a great environment for exploring these functions and working with large datasets.

Conclusion

Thanks for reading this book. If you found it helpful, please say hello on LinkedIn: http://linkedin.com/in/tekelsey

Best wishes in your learning journey.

Appendix A: Learning Areas in Python

When learning Python, focusing on the following ten areas can help you build a solid foundation and understanding of the language:

1. Syntax and Basics: Learn the basic structure of Python code, including indentation, variables, data types, operators, and simple built-in functions.
2. Control Flow: Understand conditional statements (if, elif, and else), looping structures (for and while loops), and the concept of loop control with break and continue statements.
3. Functions: Learn how to define, call, and pass arguments to functions, as well as understanding the scope of variables and the importance of return statements.
4. Data Structures: Familiarize yourself with Python's built-in data structures, including lists, tuples, sets, and dictionaries, along with their methods and common use cases.
5. File I/O: Learn how to read from and write to files, handle exceptions during file operations, and work with various file formats such as CSV and JSON.
6. Object-Oriented Programming (OOP): Understand the concepts of classes, objects, inheritance, and polymorphism, and learn how to create and use them in your Python programs.
7. Modules and Libraries: Learn how to import and use built-in and third-party modules, and explore commonly used libraries like NumPy, Pandas, and requests.
8. Error Handling and Exceptions: Understand how to handle errors and exceptions using try, except, and finally statements, and learn to create custom exception classes.
9. Testing and Debugging: Learn how to write unit tests with the unittest module or pytest, and practice using debugging tools like pdb or built-in IDE debuggers.

10. Best Practices and Code Style: Familiarize yourself with Python's style guide (PEP 8) and best practices, such as writing clear, concise, and well-documented code.

As you progress, you can explore more advanced topics, such as web development with frameworks like Flask or Django, data analysis and visualization with Pandas and Matplotlib, or machine learning with TensorFlow or scikit-learn.

Appendix B: Several ChatGPT Tips

Cut-Offs: sometimes, ChatGPT will just cut off in the middle of working on something, and often you can just type in "continue" and it will pick up where it left off.

Expand/Improve: whether you are working with standard text, or coding, ChatGPT can modify what it just worked on, including expanding, making more compact, improving, etc.

Always review: when you use ChatGPT, always review what it comes up with before passing it along, etc. Especially when it comes to asking it to write emails, analysis, etc. - you can even ask it to check itself for accuracy.

Printed in Great Britain
by Amazon